CARNAL
CHRISTIANS
IDENTITY
IN CRISIS

JANICE FOUNTAINE

ISBN: 978-1-58930-310-2

Dedication

This book is dedicated to every Christian, known and unknown, discipled and not yet discipled, titled and untitled. May we all desire to live in the dimensions of spiritual alignment with our God, our Father and our Creator that He desires and commands of us, so that we may be the true worshippers, the Remnant, the Church that our Lord and Savior Jesus Christ is coming back to receive.

Table of Contents

Acknowledgements

I acknowledge God in His sovereignty, holiness and self-existence; to whom there is no comparison or potential to compete; for besides Him there is no other.

Introduction

The pressure of conformity within our worldwide social systems of influence is pressing against Christian values in every way that it can. The doors of the family unit squeak as they cling to the loosened hinges of the Christian principles on which they are hung. Boardroom executives huddle to make life-changing decisions concerning their numerous employees, as legislative halls cleave to the sounds of politically driven changes. Our schoolhouse walls record whispers of lost innocence among our youth, while the marketplace squirms at the footsteps of sin's influences. Entertainment stages are elevated to accommodate superiority complexes, and sports fields showcase replicas of the godlike personas of those who overflow their arenas with enthusiastic fans. In the middle of it all, comprehensive behavioral centers struggle to make sense of the senselessness of man's behavior, and it ponders the lack of impact by the Christian faith upon individuals' perspectives and lifestyles regarding their creative existence within these systems.

While conformity makes no apology for its impact upon people's lives, many seemingly attached to the

Christian faith are the ones who will have to apologize. Their contribution to the continuous and uncaring application of sin's escalating blows to the strength and stability of our world's societies has, indeed, left the Christian Church in a dilemma and having to answer for much.

Thus, an alarm must be sounded to awaken the Church from her stupor and to help bring each member into a place of self-examination and correction, for the sake of the lost and for the advancement of the Kingdom of God in the earth realm.

This book, *Carnal Christians, Identity in Crisis*, is that alarm. It is a prophetic trumpet sound written to help straighten the path and awaken the wandering Christian. It is meant to give insight into the heart of God concerning the body of Christ in this season and to encourage every Christian, no matter how fivefold deep they are, to sincerely examine themselves personally and spiritually unto the Lord.

The Church's Dilemma

The Christian Church is most certainly facing a dilemma today. It is losing its savor and impact worldwide. The level of respect and effect that the Church once had has now been grossly overshadowed by the day-to-day influences and challenges of worldly systems. These systems of the world are dangerously more prevalent now in people's lives than they were in the past, including in the lives of many so-called Christians today.

The social, professional, political, and personal dynamics throughout the world are changing at a pace that is much more rapid than the rate of Christian growth and maturity. As a result, there is a constant struggle for the Church to overcome the daily impact of these changes upon the lives of Christians, and their ability to faithfully function daily, within their belief systems, which they profess to live out.

Each day, Christians must contend for their very faith, which before had been understood and accepted by most Americans as an integral part of life's daily routine. The high regard and respect for the Christian lifestyle that once existed is becoming a fading frenzy, challenged every day by people and systems of influence that had once gladly embraced it as the norm.

From the crumbling foundation of the family unit to the dungeons of partisan politics, Christianity can be seen bent over and measurably ineffective in making an impact on the lives of millions being taken captive by the diabolical wiles within the world's secular systems of influence.

Despite the Church's efforts to reinforce the evidential truths of going against the grain of one's created existence, there lain under the noses of the Apostles, Prophets, Bishops, and Pastors, the Christian Church got stuck on "pause." The biblical truths and principles of God have become buried beneath the impact of the dark, manipulative strategies existing within the world's influential systems and its undeserved allegiance of a multitude of professing Christians, known as "carnal Christians."

These carnal Christians are those who profess their love and faithfulness to the cause of Christ, yet they can be seen and heard bowing to the daily challenges of worldly influences and pivoting away from the heart of God. Yes, hidden beneath mankind's senseless allegiance to all that is not like God, lie the broken pieces of Christian faithfulness, having been deserted and now struggling to survive.

For too many Christians, worldliness is not an issue. Life must go on, yes, but it has become too much of a challenge for them each day. They are finding themselves struggling, not only with the weight of the passions and influences of earth's sophisticated life systems, but also with their relationship with God and the dynamics of the Christian Church, relative to their lives. They have begun to question the need for Christianity in such a structured form, even in the midst of an amassing self-destructive and ambiguous society and culture.

For the Church overall, this is a real problem that not only must be addressed but that must be corrected.

Yes, societal change is expected. It is normal, even necessary for growth. However; it should never seek to alter the fabric of that for which its creative purpose was once woven. While many people in our society may lack this perspective, for Christians, to deny or abandon it gives credence to the world's argument that the Christian Church is no longer vital or effective. They contend that because the people of God are now wavering in their perspective of life, both now and eternally, at heightened levels and in such astonishing ways, then they are not able to defend or live by the gospel and the principles by which they profess to live.

Unless the Church itself pivots back to God, takes a stance on His principles, and brings correction, not judgment, to its weakest link, the "carnal Christian," it, too, will become of ill effect for the cause of Christ, and the Kingdom of God will be provoked to intervene in uncharted dimensions.

Let me pause, however, and say this to all who read this book: *Carnal Christians* is not written to pass judgment on anyone, but it is by the command and grace of God that each of us would examine where we are concerning our profession of Jesus Christ and our practice of Christianity, knowing that it is God, not any natural man, who will reward us accordingly. Indeed, though, we will be rewarded.

Identity in Crisis

The most general argument that the world is making against the Christian Church today is the increasing inability of the masses to identify with them. From one end of the spectrum to the other lies a diverse variety of life perspectives that the world has neither had to explain nor needed to understand. Now each day before their very eyes appears the Christian who is looking and acting more and more like them, giving them further reason not to change their perspective.

Our identity bears witness to who we are, personally and spiritually. There are numerous factors and lifestyle dynamics that allow others to witness our identity from near or from afar. While the apostolic and prophetic reformations brought completeness to the Church's structure and a greater depth of revelation and power to the pew, there remains an untapped territory filled with spiritual carcasses, grossly lacking the echoes of Christian clarity and spiritual unity. Instead, there can be heard a resounding accentuation of an identity crisis within the body of Christ that even many Christians don't understand. It is an identity crisis that has been fueled by sin and selfishness. It is now way out of control, because of the fear of the apostolic and pastoral leadership and their refusal and inability to deal with it. In other words, there is a weakened body lurking around the presence of God, because of the leadership's failure to acknowledge and confront the attachments within the Church that are causing confusion and hindering the advancement of God's Kingdom on the earth.

The Word of God is very clear about His expectations of Christians to live by the principles of His written commands. Jesus' coming to the earth realm not only brought us back into relationship with God, but He established the ground rules for our obtaining and maintaining our position in Him on earth and our spending eternity in the presence of God. In Romans 8:29–30, Paul sums it up best: We have been predestined to be conformed to the image of Christ. Romans 12:1–2 reads: "If any man be in Christ, he is a new creature, old things are passed away and behold all things are become new."

A person's birth certificate is the comprehensive document that identifies and confirms his or her true lineage. It serves as one's past, present, and future authentication. It bears witness to a person's existence and the lifeline from which he is attached. As it is in the natural, so it is in the spiritual realm, as well. Your relationship with God is evident identification and proof of your spiritual birth and lineage.

Passports, driver's licenses, and voter registrations are all supporting documents as you progress through the world system. Each, however, would be nonexistent and without credibility except that they represent your identifiable claim that was based on your original birth certificate. The the same is also true with your lifestyle: Your principles, perspectives, and persuasions are the supporting identifiers that one can use to trace you back to your original birth.

Too many Christians are walking around without proper identification—the identification that links them back to their spiritual lineage, their place and time of birth. As a result, they are not recognizable, identifiable, or even believable. The cold, unholy world laughs at them as they are no longer stunned at their pretenses, as they say one thing and then do another. The Church bows their heads and threatens to disown them as they make true discipleship more difficult—and God? He disowns them. He refers to them as lukewarm spittle, in danger of becoming spewed out of His mouth and no longer being identified as His child.

Revelation 3:14–22 records how, when speaki to those in the church of the Laodiceans, God made known that a clear and demonstrative identity is crit to life in Him, to a relationship with Him, and to ac tance by Him. This identity must be representati who He is and His expectations of mankind relat Him. If a person cannot live by His rules, then th son cannot live by Him or remain in His presence

"And unto the angel of the church of the Laodiceans write; these things saith the Amen, the faithful and true witness, the beginning of the creation of God" (verse 14).

In other words, speaking to John, the writer of Revelation, the Lord told him to write a letter to the pastor of the church in Laodicea. Here is what the Lord asked: "Make sure he knows that I told you what to say to him to speak to the people. Say that I, the Lord thy God, the Amen, the self-established, self-existent, and sovereign truth, that I, the seen, the unseen, and the unforeseen witness of the never-ending creative existence of all things possible and impossible from everlasting to everlasting, have said…"

"I know thy works, that thou art neither cold nor hot: I would thou wert cold or hot" (verse 15).

other words, the Lord is saying, "I know the prooutcome or lack thereof, of your existence here
th realm. I am the barometer, the measuring
g   ch your works are judged. The actions of man
it   to Me, because they dictate outcomes, platcal   osing Me, and they transport vehicles of
ep   gospel, My character, My revelation, and
e of   l them that I have taken into account that
ve to   before Me, and I have come to give them
t per   of My findings. Tell them that their works
               indicative of their heart toward Me."

use thou art lukewarm, and neither cold nor
e thee out of my mouth" (verse 16).

"'Hot' means that you love Me, cold means that you don't, and lukewarm accentuates the fact that you have tried us both and have determined that at best, I am only equal in measure and worth of your love and loyalty. Meaning, you have not discovered any outstanding factors, inclusively or exclusively, that would give you a reason to declare the superiority of one or the other."

Lukewarm indicates your indecisiveness because you have neither found a convincing reason to accept nor an absolute reason to reject Christ. Lukewarm leaves people with indecision and on shaky ground. Hot or cold is saying that He has measured your efforts and have judged what has been produced by them, and that I have decided based on His measurement. Hot and cold indicates that some works exist. You have made a decision either for Him or against Him. Whether you are hot or cold, you are identifying with something. You have chosen whom you will serve. You know what you want, and what you do not want. You have made a clear choice, and as a result, you have taken on a chosen identity, either hot or cold.

But lukewarm is saying that neither is worthy of the movement of your hands. You have not chosen or taken on any identity. Therefore, the Lord is saying, you who are supposed to be His remain in crisis—an identity crisis. He has tasted of you and has found you lukewarm, and therefore He will spew you out at random, depending on the barometer of your carnality at any given point of time in your daily comings and goings. Hot or cold indicates that you at least tried at some works. Lukewarm insinuates that you never made a commitment to anything for real. I hear the Spirit of the Lord saying, "Tell them that, hot or cold, I can at least respect the effort, but lukewarm I cannot. It produces a taste in My mouth that even My saliva does not want a part of."

> *"Because thou sayest, I am rich, and increased with goods, and have need of nothing; and knowest not that thou art wretched, and miserable, and poor, and blind, and naked"*
> *(verse 17).*

The Lord is saying: "You are arrogant when you should be humble. You overestimate your depth in Me, and you underestimate where you should be in Me. You have equated material blessings with revelation and a relationship with Me. You have allowed these things to overshadow your view of Me and to give you a false interpretation of your status in the kingdom and your condition in Me. You have misinterpreted your location in Me, and you now need a supernatural GPS. Right now, you are not on the radar of eternal and everlasting life. You have allowed the figment of your imagination to give you a false sense of self-worth and your value to Me and to the kingdom advancement in the earth realm. In summary, you have a false sense of being in My presence."

> *"I counsel thee to buy of me gold tried in the fire, that thou mayest be rich; and white raiment, that thou mayest be clothed, and that the shame of thy nakedness do not ap-*

pear; and anoint thine eyes with eyesalve, that thou mayest see" (verse 18).

Praise the Lord! There is a solution to an "identity crisis"—a paradigm shift that God has provided. When you change your perspective on who brings true "value" to your life and your ways, your habits and your desires will shift. Your taste buds will then line up with what God commands for those who claim Him as Lord and Savior.

Try God! He has been tested and has been found provable. When you come to Him, you will not only recognize real value, but you will also be able to assess worth. You will find yourself wealthy beyond comparison or imagination. However; the knowledge, which is referred to in this text written by the apostle John, only comes by a revelation from God Himself. You cannot "figure it out" through any natural sense or reasoning, but only through supernatural revelation will you be able to understand your true worth, security, and pride. Only then will you see the value not only of being a Christian, but also of becoming a true worshipper in its purest form.

"As many as I love, I rebuke and chasten: be zealous therefore, and repent" (verse 19).

God will never be found lacking in His desire to restore mankind back to His original state in Him. His beckoning is endless; He knows that there is a set time for Jesus to return to the earth someday and to gather His bride, the body of Christ, for her presentation to God in purity and in honor.

Soon, multitudes of compromising Christians will face the reality of their spiritual conditions with the understanding that Jesus Christ cannot present them to the Father in an impure or marred state. The truth of the matter is that carnal Christians have a Laodicean spirit. Many, therefore, who think that they are saved in the sight of God in reality are not. Only God knows a person's true heart. The carnal Christian is missing the mark and possibly misjudging his or her position in Christ. If you are comfortable in a certain setting, then that is where your comfort is found. And where your comfort is found is indicative of where your allegiance is and who your real god is. You cannot be faithful to God, spiritually aligned with Him; while at the same time willing, habitually, and joyfully entangled in an atmosphere that is cold to Him.

Although God describes and views the indecisive and unfaithful as being separated from Him, He is still quick to practice His love for us and to show us its extent. For the disowned, disconnected, and discombobulated person, God has provided a built-in safety mechanism, a life vest, as some would describe it, for the unsaved, called *repentance*. Whichever description you choose to adopt, you can always overcome your sorrowful condition by being fervent and passionate about turning away from it.

> *"Behold, I stand at the door and knock: if any man hears my voice, and open the door, I will come into him and will sup with him, and he with me" (verse 20).*

But again, there is hope! Although God cannot change for us or because of us, He remains unchanged, as well, in being relentless in His love for us. Your ears can still process His voice, and you can still let Him in. Just open the door to your heart. God is outside waiting. If you desire to draw near to Him, He will draw near to you. And when God asks to come in, you will find that you have the strength you need to let Him in. Yes, He is still at the door knocking. His presence is still available. He is still offering you a relationship, and He still desires your fellowship. His presence is still in the earth realm, within multitudes, even at this very moment. He is willing to make you His dwelling place, and you can come to know Him in the place of life eternal and victory.

> *"To him that overcometh will I grant to sit with me in my throne, even as I also overcame, and am set down with my Father in his throne" (verse 21).*

The state of the overcomer extends far beyond this natural realm as we know it; it extends into the unseen depths of God's sovereign and holy existence. Far beyond any human reasoning, desires, or imagination, there is a dimension of the unseen (the spiritual, supernatural) realm of God that only those who overcome through the blood of the Lamb, Jesus Christ our Lord, will ever see.

Don't let the diabolical infiltrations, strategies, and "fake news" of the worldly systems of influence entice you to become a fool for it. The truth of the matter is that life exists beyond this earthly realm for every man and woman. God has wired us to live forever. Mankind exists as a three-part being: body, soul, and spirit. Because of the spirit of man, which was placed inside of us by God at our creation, our true selves, our souls, the encompassment of who we are, cannot die, but will live forever. In other words, the spirit of man keeps us alive forever. That which is a spirit, either divine or diabolical, *will* live forever in the unseen realm created by God. If you don't know God here on this earthly plane, you will know Him after your time on earth, but not in the comfort and revelatory realm of His presence. You will exist in a state of the abyss, and there is nothing that our current worldly systems of influence will be able to offer you. No, not even a cold beer or a cool glass of wine, as many sometimes suggest.

It's your decision. If you submit to the Spirit of the Lord here and now, then you will prevail and overpower that which would seek to destroy your relationship with God and control your destiny forever.

> *"He that hath an ear, let him hear what the Spirit saith unto the churches" (verse 22).*

Set your ears to hear the voice of the Lord. If you seek Him, you will recognize the voice of the Holy Spirit, and when you do, you will obey, because you will know that truly He is the Lord who speaks to you and the Church, overall.

Carnal Christian, Who Are You?

Carnal Christians have significantly contributed to the deterioration of the impact of Christianity in America and throughout the world. They cannot see this. They are so focused on their own wants and desires that they give no thought to the effect that their lifestyles have on those around them and on the kingdom of God overall. Carnal Christians lack the personal and spiritual maturity to see past themselves. They have not fully grasped the fact that holiness and faithfulness to God, without compromise, is not about being too religious, but it's about preserving the moral compass of Christianity in our society.

The word "carnal" is translated from the Greek word *sarkikos*. It means "fleshly."

Thus, the idea of a Christian being fleshly mostly refers to those persons who profess Christ, but whose lifestyles are far from being representative of their profession of faith. This leaves one to conclude only one of two things: First, either this person's behavior and lifestyle are temporary, pending their coming into the dimension of true holiness. Their carnality may be instanced by falling short of the glory of God, as many babes in Christ experience, or second, they may be an unbeliever who does not profess to be a Christian and who continuously lives a carnal lifestyle by choice, without repentance or any intention of changing. In other words, if a "carnal Christian" is genuinely saved, then sooner rather than later, he will not remain carnal any longer. He will become new through the process of sanctification, which means being spiritually set aside for God. Yes, his tendency to wander will not be habitual or by desire or by vain choice, but his lifestyle will progressively bear witness to his newness by choice of holiness and separation unto God.

Paul reminds us in Romans 12:1–2 that if any man is in Christ, he is a new creation.

So, since the implications are that the "carnal Christian" is indeed saved, the critical question to be answered is whether the carnal person was ever truly saved to begin with. Did he or she ever enter a true salvific relationship with God through Jesus Christ? This relationship is based on confession and belief, as outlined in Romans 10:9–10, a confession and belief that only God and perhaps that person can truly confirm.

First John 2:19 lets us know that true repentance causes a person to stay in fellowship with Jesus Christ rather than to leave it. It states, "They went out from us, but they were not of us; for if they had been of us, they would no doubt have continued with us: but they went out, that they might be made manifest that they were not all of us."

I want to emphasize, so as not to discourage the "babes in Christ" who are reading this message, or to give them a reason for procrastination, that the writing of *Carnal Christians* is most relative to the so-called seasoned Christians. I am referring to those who have been around long enough to know and do better for the cause of Christ. These men and women have found a way around Christianity and its biblical principles to the point that they have convinced themselves that they can easily live a carnal lifestyle, especially in specific areas of their lives. They in turn try to "make up for it" by living a Christian lifestyle in another area, professing Christianity hypocritically rather than as a reality in their lives.

They profess Christ, but they are not practicing the principles of worship and holiness before God in the depth that they need to practice them in order to be assured eternal and everlasting life in the presence of God. Nor would they be able to carry His glory and receive His end-time anointing for the demonstration of His power in the earth realm in these latter days.

From the pulpit to the pew, and into the hearts and homes of many churchgoers, the roving eye of the carnal Christian can be clearly seen. Pastoral teachings and exhortations, more often than not, are being overshadowed by worldly temptations, illicit relationships, the elevation of public sentiments, political rhetoric, media frenzies, special interest groups and so-called holy leaders who profess to be men and women of God but who are far from it.

First Peter 1:15–16 states: "But as he which hath called you is holy, so be ye holy in all manner of conversation; Because it is written, Be ye holy; for I am holy." This means that we must always be ready to promote God and defend the gospel of the kingdom with a mature answer and a response to all things. This answer must be based on godly principles and spoken by one who has a separated and an anointed lifestyle of living and walking in the holiness and power of God on a daily basis. God expects us to live and spread the gospel of His kingdom, which is based on the birth, life, ministry, death, resurrection, ascension, and future coming of Jesus Christ relative to this earth and the supernatural realms and dimensions of God.

The Weakest Link

Perhaps one of the biggest enemies of the Christian Church today is the Church itself. Within the walls and beneath the pillars and the pews of Christianity's segment of the religious system, one can hear the chatter of those who profess to be Christians and to love God. On the outside, they are Church workers, servant-leaders of the Most High God and a necessary part of His kingdom. However, on the inside, they have an unstable and double-minded type of vision. They are living with the tendency to wander from one place to another. It is as if they are stuck between two worlds. In reality, this is a conscious choice, often backed by the argument that the Church is either too religious, is not up-to-date, cannot relate to real people, is too judgmental, or is simply stuck in the past. In other words, God is too demanding, too hard on sin.

The interpretation of God's principles cannot be based on independent interpretation, nor can it be done in the context of our emotions or desires. It must be done without compromise, without prejudice or pomp and circumstance.

Unless a person taps into certain dimensions of the presence and the revelatory knowledge of God, he will not be able to overcome the influance from the secular systems' reign of sin and its impact upon his life. The depth of the spiritual implications and their involvement in the lives of man is unimaginable. Its dimensions are not birthed out of the natural realm, but out of the spirit, and therefore they far exceed anything that we can handle naturally.

For faithful and committed Christians, worldly entanglement is not a game, nor is it anything that can be taken lightly. To disciple the lost, we must have influence, which is hinged on our being in a relationship with God and staying in fellowship with Him.

Carnal Christians don't understand the spiritual presence and influence found throughout the secular systems of the world. Many of their minds shift, and their thoughts wander into uncharted battlegrounds of the supernatural that they can neither understand nor explain.

Consequently, they can easily become recklessly entangled in the moments, the movements, and the mindsets of the ungodly, and the one who once professed to be a Christian is now seen as hopelessly yielding to the ways and doings that are directly opposite to the principles of God—the very principles that they had once professed as the prevailing cause and strength of their faithful lifestyles.

These carnal Christians are without the revelation of who God is in respect to everything that is going on in and around them. They turn a blind eye to their need to tap into the One who is the Source of their being and their salvation, the One who should be the object of their worship.

Carnal Christians are unchecked, unchallenged, and unholy. These are the resounding words that emphasize the complaints of many true worshippers before the Lord: "When are the Church leaders going to deal with those carnal Christians? Lord, please bring Your correction to the carnal Christian soon! They are loose cannons within Your body. They shoot off their mouths in vulnerable places and are wreaking havoc. They are a loose segment of the Church that has not yet been approached. They are Your Church's weakest link."

The truth of the matter is that the committed, hardworking, kingdom-minded, holy, soul focused disciples really want to say: "Carnal Christians, please go and sit down somewhere else. Please! You are making our jobs harder and harder each day. As a matter of fact, just go and find yourself a deeper place in the worship realm of God. You are confused, and you are confusing those around you. You don't bring glory to God.

"You underestimate the height of God's expectations for holiness and His displeasure in your behavior. You downplay His willingness to chastise you and bring you into correction. And you overestimate the depth of your relationship and growth and maturity in the Lord.

"You put blinders over the hearts of the broken with your selfishness. Your lack of depth in the purpose, presence, and power of God, beyond your worldly appetites, has caused even you yourself to walk in darkness, especially concerning His heart for the broken and the unsaved.

"Your hardened heart has wandered into a carnal lifestyle that only has respect for what God can do for you, while you walk in darkness concerning the heartbeat of God about His kingdom advancing in the earth.

"I am not judging you. I don't need to. Your fruit is sufficient proof. Who you are is clear—you are carnal—and who you are not—holy—is even more clear.

"You make the job harder for those who truly walk in holiness. You 'hold the truth down in unrighteousness.'

"You support the principles of God only if they don't go against the grain of your favorite politician, TV show, entertainer, dance, drink, curse word, or habit.

"You pick and choose what parts of God you want and you find an excuse to support your rejection of what parts you don't want. You try to claim holiness in one area while you remain unchanged in all of the other areas.

"You make our jobs so much harder, not because you don't agree with me, not because you don't see what I see, and not because you reject the deeper depths of God that would give you clarity and bring holiness to your lifestyle, but because you are so confusing to the broken person watching you or listening to the warmth of your double-mindedness whom I am trying to disciple.

I am trying to point them to the cross, and you are pointing them to happy hour. Please, go and sit down somewhere so that they may live.

"While we uncompromising Christians are on the job with the Lord, witnessing to the truth, you are trying to justify your unholiness by saying something else that is totally contrary to God. Go sit down and be quiet, please!"

You can sugarcoat it all you want , but God is not taking you like that. You must be presentable to Him.

The Obvious Question

Carnal Christian! *Do you even want to be a Christian?* Why not just drop the suit and live in the world without the confession? I mean, what difference does it make? As long as you are happy, right? I mean, it's not like you were fooling or convincing anyone else anyway. You spend your time impressing the world and defending yourself and mocking other Christians as if they are your enemies. No one is fooled by your pretense. The world knows that you act and look and talk like them, and other Christians know that you *don't* look and act and talk like them, and you—deep inside of you—know that you are faking it in both areas. You pretend to be worldly around the worldly, and you pretend to be a Christian around Christians. And in doing so, you don't completely relate to either. You feel left out during times of extreme or uncompromising proof. You find yourself an outcast at the time. You don't totally fit in in either arena and you are not totally accepted by either group. When it gets too hot in either direction, you profess that you belong to or are a part of the other group. You have boundaries on both sides. You fit in until you don't want to fit in anymore, until it is no longer convenient or beneficial to you. In reality, you are an outcast, unidentifiable. You may be alive and breathing, but you are unidentifiable. People don't really know where you came from, yet they know that you belong or should be somewhere else. The truth of the matter, though, is that you appear as one having amnesia, not knowing which direction to go, directionless, not knowing who you really are or where you really belong.

No one can tell who you are by your dress because it's confusing, by your speech because it's confusing, nor by your appearance because it's confusing, too. No one, including yourself, recognizes you as completely a part of them or fully theirs, because they neither witnessed any authentic commitment from you nor experienced any genuine fellowship with you. All that they can really say is that you are experiencing an identity crisis, because no one really knows who you are, not even yourself.

It appears that there are many Carnal Christians who have neither the troubled soul in mind nor Christianity of which they confess to be an intricate part. They seen to have only a selfish, self-serving desire to exist in both realms of society. Part of the problem is that the Christian Church herself is stuck in an identity crisis. From the pulpit to the front door of the church, many are finding themselves in a weak and vulnerable position relative to their wants and desires and what the Church and the world have to offer. As a result, there are many people torn between two loves depending upon what day it is, what mood they are in, and which system—the world or the Church—has the most to offer them at the time.

"I am not carnal, but I am not religious either" is the declaration of many who fit the description of a carnal Christian.

We are now in a time when more and more Christians are being labeled "abnormal," as they are faced with the decision of whether or not to engage in or support issues or behavioral lifestyles that were before clearly understood and accepted as being ungodly. The outcome of these decisions is contributing to our country witnessing a weakened, divided, indecisive, and desensitized Christian base. Now when a colleague, friend, or loved one requests support on generally accepted non-Christian issues, Christians face the fear of losing these relationships, hurting someone they care about, or even seeing the relationship completely severed if they choose not to support their friend in an area that conflicts with Christian principles. For many Christians, this is a problem. Oftentimes, it becomes a life-changing problem because the support being sought does not line up with traditional godly principles by which Christians live and exist. The average person seeks to provide their acquaintances or loved ones with the support that they need during various critical times in their lives. But many Christians have become desensitized at an alarming pace and are now deciding to give support on issues that they were not traditionally expected to or even exposed to. To sum it up, the rate of social change in our society has caused many Christians to become desensitized about issues that, until now, they would not have ever considered supporting. But for the sake of their relationships with family, friends, and even themselves, many have abandoned the godly principles that they once professed.

"Religious" has been the word used to describe the Christian who seems to go too far in his or her beliefs. "Extremists," "holy rollers," "Jesus freaks," "self-righteous," and the like all roll off the tongues of their many accusers. Both Christians and non-Christians argue that the "religious Christian" is of no earthly good, that these people need to loosen up and relax. Their actions may become so extreme that they are not representative of Christ. They may fail to clearly articulate, represent, and demonstrate the love of God and the principles they profess and are commanded to live by. As a matter of fact, it has been contended that the problem with the Christian Church is the "religious" Christian who lives in holiness without compromise.

However, there are those who choose to respond to such allegations, especially to those who proclaim to love God and live by His principles. They begin by defining religious, according to Webster, as simply meaning relating to or believing in a religion.

"You say that I am religious, yet I say that you are not religious enough. You say that I take God too seriously, yet I say that you don't take Him seriously enough. You say that I don't relate to the world, yet I say that the world doesn't relate to me. You say that I am too different, yet I say that I am supposed to be different. You say that I am too religious, yet I say that you don't know who you are. In actuality, *you* are in an identity crisis."

It is true that as Christians, we must understand that trials, temptations, and tribulations of the world are integrated into the world system and have become an everyday influential presence in the lives of men, women, and even children, worldwide. Our understanding must seep into the depths of life's realities and bring to people a new answer and its way out. However, many Christians have taken this to mean intermingling within the secular systems and becoming like and as those whom we have been called to lead.

I will admit that within the Christian religious sector, some Christians walk in an unlearned, unseasoned, and unled dimension of discipleship in which they err in their intentions and in their implementation of exposing God and making the gospel of the kingdom appeal to those who have not come into the knowledge and safety of a true, uncompromising walk with God. As a result, many have walked away with a bitterness toward Christianity, even more confused about their lives than before and vowing never to have such an intense interaction again. They label the Church or Christians as uncaring, unloving, and unable to relate to what they are experiencing. And rightly so, according to what they may have experienced from the one or ones whom they encountered. However, just as eager is the Christian whom they will encounter and who will usher them into a life-changing, everlasting relationship as they come to know Christianity, through fellowship and encounters with the Lord and other more learned and skillful Christians.

The damage that may have been done to the unsaved person, however, cannot begin to compare with the damage that the carnal Christian is doing to them and to the cause of Christ on a daily basis. Some of this damage is caused ignorantly and some is caused by those who simply don't care.

Consider That the Broken Cry

Demands of God to be holy, the cries of the lost to be changed, the tears of the broken and the lost—all are crying unto God for deliverance from the vicious bondage of sin. Many are finding themselves up against a force that is far superior to them. In essence, the lost don't want to be lost, but they don't know the way out nor do they have the strength to come out without assistance. They need the Church, which has been equipped by God to usher them into a safe place of fellowship and existence.

This condition of the broken and the lost is bringing an indictment against the Christian Church. It charges that the people of God have been missing in action and are viewed as being unholy, weak, compromising, lacking self-control, self-engrossed, uncommitted, and unfaithful to God. This is an indictment that often does not go without warrant or witness.

The present condition of the world is dictating the brevity that we as Christians must consider with relation to our overall Christian walk and where God wants us to be. This is no game. This is no plaything. This is life at its most serious. Everyone who professes to be a Christian must reconsider the depth of their own spirituality in comparison to the height of God's expectations for them.

The Church must consciously measure the seriousness of what is happening in the world with respect to Christianity. When you think that you are being compassionate, oftentimes you are being drawn into a web of deception that, not only may you never get out of, but that the innocent ones whom you are taking with you may never get out.

This is a time when the Christian confession is being challenged and questioned. Every Christian, no matter how deep they think they are, must find themselves in a deeper place in God, and they must not come out of that place. They must seriously and sincerely tap in to worship realms and dimensions that they have never experienced before. This is growth time. We must hear from God on what is taking place in our society, and this is going to require a deeper level of revelation and depth in the presence of God than we currently have. The body of Christ cannot afford to miss this. We are dealing with a God who has been provoked to gather a remnant. We must move into a deeper dimension in God and hear from Him like never before, so that we will not miss His move in our world today.

How is it so seemingly easy for you, who so elegantly grace the pews and the pulpits, the choir stands, the radio stations, and the television sets from to Sunday to Sunday, to veer off the road of godly principles that you profess to follow as a Christian? Are you really willing to jeopardize your eternal position in Christ? Are you really willing to gamble with the souls of the unregenerate and the unsaved? Who are you that you would snatch their lives from the security of salvation and dangle them over the fire of improbability? How is it that you are not strong enough to contend for the faith? How is it that you are not strong enough to hold to the profession of your faith without wavering? How is it that you are not tapping in to the revelation realms of the essence and the being of God and allowing Him to speak into your spirit a truth that deep down you already know to be? How is it that you, men and women of God, can dwell in the comfort zones of your own Christianity and not give serious thought to the impact that you are having on the futures of the unsaved and on the Christian faith? How is it that you can jeopardize Christianity itself for your own weakness and frailty in the faith? How is it that it seems to be easier for you to justify the wrong than it is to for you to defend the right?

This, people of God, is too serious of a charge for you to be selfish. You cannot afford to miss God. You are putting your eternal resting place in question. "Be not decieved; God is not mocked: for whatsoever a man soweth, so shall he also reap".

I hear God asking, "How did you become so fragile O Body? How did you become so timid and weak? How did you become so far from Me that I cannot even recognize Myself in you? Return to Me and know who I am. I am the One who birthed you. I made you. You are My people. Return to Me. Return to Me. I know who you are. You are Mine. Return to Me and know that I am the Lord your God."

Remember, body of Christ. We are the objects of God's affection, and He longs to be the object of ours.

Carnal, but Beloved Shepherds

I hear the Spirit of the Lord saying that many Pastors have forgotten that He is a holy God and a God of order: "The sheep have gone astray, and no one wants to be accountable. But you, you whom I have made to be Shepherds over My flock, have turned them away from Me, and now you yourself must turn from your wicked ways, or else I will come. And I will take the stench from their nostrils. The stench of sin. For I am a holy God. Holy, I am, and I require holiness from you. You do not teach them My ways, but there are ways of your own that you desire, and you teach them those ways. You teach them as if those ways are of Me. Know that they are a stench to My nostrils and that, therefore, you have become a stench to Me. Today, this day, teach them that they are My own. I know them, and I love them. I will not share them with another."

I pray that the Pastors reading this, the Shepherds of any fivefold persuasion who are ruling over the flock, will realize that God is not playing with us. Those who lead and who are led, we all have responsibilities to God, and we each will be held accountable for our deeds before Him.

Romans 1:18 reads: "For all have sinned and come short of the glory of God." We must each give an account of our lives before Him. We who are sheep will not be able to blame the shepherd for our not having lived up to our responsibilities before God. Yes, sure, many have failed, and God will deal with them, but there are those who sit under them because of the convenience of sin. Yes, it is convenient for you when the pastor is unholy, because you, too, are unholy and it gives you an excuse to be unholy, as well. Oh yes, if the shepherd has a loose tongue, a wandering eye, or a taste for wine and other spirits, then you give him a pass because it gives you a pass to sin, as well.

The reason so many pastors continue in their state of sin is that the congregation does not want to lose them. Many would rather lose God Himself than their beloved pastor, who leads them on a path of sin rather than holds them accountable. So, the Church continues to thrive in carnality rather than exist in holiness before God. Many so-called Christians would rather be out of fellowship with God than be without their beloved pastor. As for me, I would rather be in God's world without you, than in your world without Him.

From one pastor to another, I pray that you would come into a place where you understand the seriousness of leading people into a clear and mature path in the Lord.

Carnal Christians are surface believers. They lack the depth necessary to carry them through a heavy battle in the spirit realm. They have failed to seek God in a deeper dimension outside of their pastor's Sunday morning service. This lack of diligence has birthed cluelessness, carnality, and unidentifiable Christians.

You are turning a blind eye to the carnal, and some of you are the reason many Christians are carnal in the first place, because they are following you, to whom they have entrusted their souls. Silence is not an option when God is commanding you to sound the trumpet. You are to blame as well. First, you sit back and say nothing. You provide neither contention for the faith nor help for the faithless.

Then you sit back and complain about the way things are. How can you demonstrate the Word of God or bring clarity of His will to a dying world, if you never hear their cries or if they never hear your voice?

Leaders who use the Bible to justify their own sinful lifestyles and behavior are placing themselves in the range of God's discipline and judgment. They are tampering with the souls of the unlearned who are crying for the truth. And in the midst of it all, they are giving them a lie.

You, sir, you, ma'am, will one day have to answer to God. Many of you wear your priestly robes and flash your bishop's rings while hiding the fact that you are struggling with unholy behavior and lifestyles yourself. You will be held accountable to God for any lack of faith in believing that He will deliver and bring you out of any place that you have found yourself intertwined and that probably requires a greater depth of faith than you currently have.

If you allow Him to do so, God will take every part of His Word and make it applicable to your healing and deliverance. He will place you in a safe environment and not let you out until you are strong enough to contend with that which has entangled you and caused you to be bound.

But instead, your reliance on private interpretation for selfish motives are leading you and many others to a place of no return. You have caused many who would have followed you into the halls of deliverance, to instead be drawn into the tunnels of eternal damnation. And you, pastor, will pay a heavy price to God for those souls who were lost.

Your sheep deserve better. They know not the spiritual aspects of their struggles. But you, pastor, have tapped into the supernatural realms of the existence of God. You have tapped into a depth in Him in which you know deep down that there is more. You have yielded to your flesh and kept the reality and holiness of God a secret during times when people needed to know the truth the most.

Yes, deep within, you knew the truth, yet you lied for the sake of satisfying your own fleshly tendencies, habits, and desires. You raked people over the coals and have now left them there to burn. You, pastor, have failed God, and you have failed those whom you have misled, and now you boast as if you have helped them. Well, you have not. You have misled generations into thinking that God will condone that which He hates. God detests deviance from His character, His laws, and His principles. You, pastor, have resonated a voice from the Church that should have never been heard.

Accept the Truth

The facts may change, but the truth remains. It is what it is when it comes to God. It is saying that facts are based on man's reasoning, understanding, and agreement, that they are what they are, but the real truth, the truth of God, is not based on our understanding. We may have the ability to rationalize, but the truth, supernatural truth, is what it is because God said so.

Supernatural truth is according to the will and the Word of God. Whether or not we "agree" or "disagree," the truth is that nothing is or is not unless God says so.

So, just because you want to believe that it is okay to say, to do, or support the practice of something that you alone or that you and your friend, co-worker, family member, yoga partner, dance partner, prayer partner, or anyone else believes is okay, does not make it a relative, relevant, or reliable fact. It is only "factual" among yourselves; it has no merit outside of you and yours. At the end of the day, the unholy decisions we make, the choices we make, the parts we play in life, are only good for us and those whom we either have influence over or who are influencing us. It is that which God, our Creator, has deemed to be contrary to the existence and behavior of those of us whom He has created. The temporary enjoyment, pleasure, satisfaction, and enlightenment of you "being you," despite the truths that God has laid down, cannot begin to compare with the joy that He has promised in this dimension of life and in the incorruptible one to those who acknowledge and live by His truth. At the end of the day, no, you cannot afford to miss God. Neither can I. No one can.

The truth is what it is.

Jesus was full of grace and truth.

The truth is that holiness is a requirement of God. And without it, no man shall see Him. Aside from this, the facts, our independent, rational, or irrational beliefs are irrelevant, are without merit, and have no weight.

The truth is that God's principles, by which we are commanded to live, are what we must follow, whether or not we think they are too hard or too harsh.

The truth is, you are the inferior, created being, and God is your superior Creator.

The truth is, our bodies are the temples of God, and we don't get to use them without a sense of responsibility or destroy them without facing accountability.

The truth is, you are struggling with sin.

The truth is, you relate to the world more than you relate to God.

The truth is, you relate more to people who live by worldly principles than you relate to those who live by God's principles.

The truth is, everyone knows the truth about you, but you are either in denial or you don't care.

The truth is, Jesus Christ is coming back soon for His Church, and that can include you and me, but we must be without spot or wrinkle.

The truth is, there is no oil in your lamp, even though you know that the Bridegroom is coming.

The truth is, there may be second chances in life, but there are no second chances to live. We only get one. After this, the resurrection. Glory to God! If you live your life abiding in His truth, then a greater dimension of life and His presence awaits you.

The Carnal Remedy

It is ultimately a **love** issue. It takes a supernatural dimension of love to deny the things of the world. Love is a complex concept in our society, but it is the true all, the greatest measuring rod in a relationship. It can define it, redefine it, and even destroy it, but at the end of the day, it is the most quantitative and defining factor in one's life when describing the faithfulness and when measuring the depth and responsibility of the relationship. As it is in the natural, so it is in the spiritual. Our relationship with God is demonstrated by our depth of love for Him and our obedience to Him, our sacrifice unto Him, our respect for, love of and worship of Him. It all can be measured by this same tool, love. And while our love for Him can be expressed in words and released through deeds, the treasure-trove that it is in no way reflects or expresses His love for us or the benefits that we receive for loving Him. In other words, love in its natural dimension, does not have the capability nor the potential to penetrate the influence of sin upon our lives. Unless we are willing to increase our worship to aquire God's supreme depth of this emotion, the sacrifice of our lives and the submission of our will that is necessary to overcome the delight of sin will only find us in a place where we fall short of the holiness required by God, and that is necessary to please Him. We must tap in to a greater depth and understanding of God to fall into this sphere of love and devotion to Him.

If you don't put this into practice, you will never be able to recognize the gravity of His love nor will you touch the surface of His holiness. You will never come to know the joy of living before Him without compromise to sin. There is an innate ability within us to love God, but this must surface out of our desire to know Him. This is why Paul says in 1 John 4:4b that... greater is He who is in us than he who is in the world. We are tapped in to the ability to overcome anything in the natural realm that challenges or seeks to usurp any influence and authority over our lives that is outside of God and His will for us.

Carnality is nothing new, but it is still prohibited by God. While mankind remains the same on this issue, God also remains the same. He will not change and cannot change, in order to remain sovereign and holy, especially unto Himself.

There are so many issues that Christians differ on, but the truth of the matter and the reality of it all is that God's principles as expressed in His Word are clear.

Many claim to have come to a revelation that would support a compromise, but all so-called revelation must be supported by His written Word, and vice versa.

Revelation is the supernatural insight into the depth and being of God. It creates spiritual activity that will bring forth a spoken word or a nonverbal act by man or by angels. Paul said in 1 Corinthians 33:1a, "Though I speak with the tongue of men and angels..." There is language and activity that we have been given privy to and are able to express as a result of revelation or an unveiling that prompts an action, word, or activity. Once an individual comes into a certain dimension of revelation, he, as Paul stated in Hebrews 6:4-6, cannot go back from God. The one who has delighted in and tasted of God will never return to his old ways as a delight. This supernatural dimension into the revelation of God is birthed out of a desire to love and know Him. And only God can bring you into this place, because He has set the standard.

Many people don't understand that the political, entertainment, science, technology, and other systems of influence do not align themselves with our Creator, so that which they produce is naturally opposite and offensive to Him. So, for one to be attached to the appetites of these systems is a clear indication of misalignment, mistaken identity, and misplaced love. Yes, you may love something, but it's not of God.

In Closing

You cannot be holy and worldly at the same time. Holiness self-exists as a distinction within itself. What I mean is that, when worldliness is practiced, then holiness no longer exists. So, you can only strive for the one or the other. Unless you maintain a constant stride toward holiness in love, peace, patience, integrity, etc., without desiring to mix with the filth and dangers of worldliness, you will never come to experience the greatness of holiness or the awe of your created existence, which is far greater than any worldly entanglement and is revealed in the sovereign and creative power and perfection of God—not gods, but the only true and living One, Jehovah God.

His depths are so far-reaching that our natural mind and our natural hand cannot begin to understand or reach Him without His grace to comprehend it. This grace comes through a divine release by God Himself. Many non-Christians will not understand. Don't expect them to. Just know that wherever you are in your relationship with God, you must embrace a deeper place in Him. Not only will you have a greater understanding of the seriousness of this book, but most importantly, you will come to know and also understand the heart and movements of God in a deeper dimension as you strive to fulfill His purpose for you.

God's will is to gather His people for kingdom advancement and for them to pursue eternal and everlasting life by believing in His existence and sovereignty. They will come to know Him in the depths of His divinity. One God, one body, one power, and one Victor will spring forth in the hearts and minds of a lost and dying world, and then and only then, will we behold the fullness of the presence and glory of God, from everlasting to everlasting.

This will encompass those who profess to believe in God to live uncompromising lives, all to His glory and to the advancement of His purposes on earth.

The Church has for far too long been laughed at and mocked as being powerless, unholy, unrighteous, unable to relate, and out of touch with the broken and the lost. It is time for us to step up to the plate and be about God's business without wavering. It's as if we are at bat, in the bottom of the ninth inning, behind and with no one on base. We must get it together—now.

The realms of God can only be entered through the process of worship and impartation. The glory realm, which is the expression of the fullness of God, cannot be accessed without going through certain depths or dimensions of worship. Anyone can witness these demonstrations and manifestations of glory, but only certain ones will live, move, and operate in the glory realm. These are those who have tapped into the dimensions of worship that excel and propel the Christian into an unchartered, immeasurable, and unimaginable lifestyle, relationship, and fellowship with God.

The average Christian should know how to recognize the diabolical and divine activities and movements in the world, especially in relation to their daily living, personally and throughout the secular systems of the world. This is a dimension that Christians must tap into spiritually, so that they may be privy to the wiles of the devil and become steadfast and effective soldiers for the cause of Christ. They must not allow man's reasoning to draw them away from that which they know God has called holy. God is neither a man nor an idol that He should lie. His Word is what He says it is. A person cannot allow themselves to be led astray and then expect God to bless them while they rest in that very thing that they have allowed to lead them astray. You must ask yourself, What is it inside of me that has caused me to abandon the very principles of God upon which Christianity was built, and upon which my covenant with God is based? You cannot be led into another realm and then expect God to smile upon that which you know is wrong, that which is contrary to the principles and commandments found in His Word.

We must be stronger during life's challenges. We must not allow the winds and the waves of deception to continue beating against the very fabric of Christianity and causing the Church to self-destruct. You who lack revelation knowledge will be an intricate ally to this deception. In Hosea 4:6, God said: "My people perish for the lack of knowledge." Spiritual knowledge involves coming into revelatory realms of God and finding out what He is saying at any given time and in any given place. It is tapping into the depth of God's being and hearing what the Lord is saying.

Prayer for the Carnal

O Lord, sanctify Your people unto You. Bring them into the reality of themselves, relative to the realm of mankind's existence and our relation to You, our everlasting Father. Help us all to know the greatness of Your sovereign realm of existence and that life in Your presence far exceeds anyone or anything on earth. Grant us a supernatural shift that will accommodate the eyes of our understanding and the lack of revelation thereof. Open the eyes of our understanding, shift our view, and allow the carnal Christian to see You in a greater depth and on a new horizon.

For all is unto You, Lord. All is unto You. In Jesus Christ's name. Amen.

Lord, I declare that the carnal shall receive this release of fire upon their spirits as their eyes sink into the words of this prayer. Cause Your voice to resonate throughout their spirits, and cause their ears to become open to the sound of Your trumpet, bidding them to return, and to hear the knock of Your hand upon the doors of their hearts. Cause Your Spirit winds to blow briskly across the floodgates of their minds, as they repent and cry out for the depths of Your revelation, presence, and glory upon their prostrate spirits in prayer and worship. Shift, winds, shift. North wind, take your stance, for the glory of the Lord is shining upon the carnal Christian who has opened his heart to the Lord. Spirit of fire, release them now in Your everlasting glory and power and honor, unto the Lord. For He is holy, and His holiness shall be forever and forever. Amen.

A Carnal Christian's - Prayer of Repentance

Oh Lord, My God, how excellent is thy name.

In the name of Jesus Christ, Father God I pray your forgiveness for my sins before you. I confess that I have not kept my promises to you; to live holy before you always, even despite what has taken place in my past, or who is before me now. No Lord, I have neither represented you to the best of my ability, nor to the extent of my potential according to my knowledge and profession of you.

Yes, Father, I am sorry. I know that I have sinned against you. I want to get it right. I want to do better. I want to live in holiness, because you established it. You command it and you expect it. Hebrews 12:14 tells me to; Follow peace with all men, and holiness, without which no man shall see the Lord. Furthermore, Romans 1:18 is read; For the wrath of God is revealed from heaven against all ungodliness and unrighteousness of men, who hold the truth in unrighteousness.

Father, I pray also, for those who have witnessed my transgressions against you. I am sorry that some *may have stumbled, fallen and even rejected you, because of what they saw and heard from me and because of what they did not see or did not hear me say that they should have concerning you and the lifestyle of an authentic Christian. I could have shown them the love of the only true and sovereign God, but instead I showed them the love of the world. I could have taught them how to live holy but instead they saw how to live carnal. I could have exposed you to them, but instead I exposed them to that which is contrary. I could have shown them how to keep your commandments and to live by your principles, but instead I exhibited ungodly principles. I could have helped them, instead I hurt them. God, I am sorry. Forgive me, I pray.*

Bring me Father, into the dimension of love unto you that will cause me to reject carnality and worldly temptations, and cling to you and your will for me, at all times. In Jesus Christ's name, I thank you Father and I pray. Amen

Order & Contact Information

jfountaineministries@gmail.com
www.janicefountaine.org